Doing the right thing!

Learning Unlimited's
'Literacy for Active Citizenship' series

Written by Monica Eguez
Photos by Monica Eguez

Learning Unlimited

Doing the right thing!

Published by Learning Unlimited.

Foreword

Learning Unlimited's 'Literacy for Active Citizenship' series

The graded readers in the 'Literacy for Active Citizenship' series are for adults who are settling in the UK, who are speakers of other languages (ESOL) and who are still developing their skills in English and in reading.

The first 20 titles in this series were produced as part of the EU-funded Active Citizenship and English (ACE) project, led by Learning Unlimited (2013 – 2015). The ACE project supported migrant women to develop their skills and confidence in English and to take an active part in everyday life in the UK. We wanted to use the real-life experiences of our learners and volunteers in a writing strand of the project to support adult migrants settling in the UK. These stories, written by ESOL learners and volunteers who supported them, include funny, personal and less typical aspects of everyday life in the UK.

The new titles in this series are also written by learners and volunteers from Learning Unlimited's programmes. These include a range of learner stories, including some about more serious topics such as crime and health.

All the stories have been edited by ESOL specialists at Learning Unlimited. There are two versions of each story – Entry 1 (A1) and Entry 2+ (A2+) supported by free downloadable materials from the Learning Unlimited website: **www.learningunlimited.co/publications/esolreaders**

We hope you enjoy the 'Literacy for Active Citizenship' series.

My name is Monica and I am
from Ecuador.
I speak Spanish.
I live in London.
My husband is French.
We have two beautiful girls.
Alicia is five years old and
Sofia is two years old.

I speak Spanish to the children.
My husband speaks French to them.
We worry about this.

I go to a course at a Children’s Centre.
The course is for families with
different languages.

I learn a lot of things.
It is good to speak your own language
to your children.
It is easy for children
to learn many languages.
Children do not mix up
different languages.
I am happy to learn this!

I learn that it is good to celebrate your culture with your children.

It is Sofia's christening.
We decorate the house with pink balloons and angels.
We eat a lot of Ecuadorian food.
We speak English, Spanish and French.

I tell everyone, “Speak your language to your children!”

When we go to Ecuador, our children speak Spanish.
When we go to France, our children speak French to their grandparents.
At school in England, Alicia speaks English like an English child.

I am proud of my children.
They speak Spanish, French and English.
I am doing the right thing!

Key words

angel	
christening	give a baby their name in church
course	some lessons
decorate	make something look pretty
mix up	think something is something else
proud	feel good about something
worry	to be unhappy about something and think too much about it

Questions

1. Where are Alicia and Sophia's parents from?

2. What languages do they speak?

3. Where is the course Monica goes to?

4. Why do Sophia's parents decorate the house?

5. What languages do the children speak to their grandparents?

Talk in pairs

6. What languages do you speak in your family?

7. How do you decorate your home for a special celebration?

Activity 1

What languages does your family speak?

Write about the languages you and your family use.

1. I can speak ....

2. At home we speak ....

3. When I go shopping I speak ....

For more downloadable activities, visit:
www.learningunlimited.co/publications/esolreaders

Acknowledgements

Doing the right thing! was written by Monica Eguez and illustrated by Monica Eguez's photos. We are grateful to the Eguez family for being able to include their story as part of the 'Literacy for Active Citizenship' series.

Doing the right thing! was edited by Karen Dudley, Judy Kirsh, Julia McGerty, Tessa Giffin, Foufou Savitzky and Sarah Sheldon at Learning Unlimited.

Angel icon made by Darius Dan from www.flaticon.com
Designed by Daisy Dudley www.daisydudley.com